SPIRITUAL
AWARENESS

From Darkness to Light

ISLAND PRINCESS

WESTBOW
P R E S S®
A DIVISION OF THOMAS NELSON
& ZONDERVAN

WestBow Press books may be ordered through booksellers or by contacting:

WestBow Press
A Division of Thomas Nelson & Zondervan
1663 Liberty Drive
Bloomington, IN 47403
www.westbowpress.com
844-714-3454

Scripture taken from the King James Version of the Bible.

ISBN: 978-1-6642-3272-3 (sc)
ISBN: 978-1-6642-3271-6 (e)

Library of Congress Control Number: 2021915654

Print information available on the last page.

WestBow Press rev. date: 8/5/2021

This book is dedicated to everyone who has experienced these types of spiritual events in their lives and came through victoriously, and those who are still fighting their way through.

Contents

Acknowledgments

First, I want to thank my Lord and Savior Jesus Christ for using me as a vessel to show his love for everyone. I was inspired to write this book because I realize that God gives us testimonies to share with others so we can tell them how great God really is to us. The experiences in my life help to define who I am and my relationship with God.

This book is written for anyone who truly believes in our Lord and Savior Jesus Christ. "If ye shall ask any thing in my name, I will do it" (John 14:14). I believe God has the power to do anything and will go any length for those who love him and call on his name:

> And it shall come to pass that all who call upon the name of the LORD shall be delivered; for in Mount Zion and in Jerusalem there shall be those who escape, as the LORD has said, and among the survivors shall be those whom the LORD calls. (Joel 2:32)

1

Childhood Experiences

As a young child, I lived with my grandmother most of the time. My grandmother was a religious woman. Each morning, she and I would worship. We sang songs like "Just as I Am without One Plea," read the Bible lessons that we got from church each week, and read Bible passages, such as, "The Lord is my shepherd I shalt not want" (Psalm 23:1). She explained everything to me. She always told me to love God, put him first in my life, and never forget to pray. I learned to trust and believe in God as I saw him operate in my life. Whenever I had trouble in my life, I would get down on my knees and pray. Sometimes I would run up the hillside, climb a tree, and talk with God about all the things that were troubling me. Before I would leave the tree, I would receive my answer from God. And I then left the hillside singing with joy in my heart because I knew that God had answered my prayer.

Sometimes I would lay in my grandmother's bed and have this vision of evil spirits fighting me, talking with me, and leading me astray. The vision would appear as a dark shadow, and then suddenly, God would appear as a bright light with a soft, still voice. Then I would see Satan and God wrestling in the garden above the house, but I never saw who won. I had these visions until I was twenty-three and gave my life to God.

2

Awareness

When I was a child, my favorite subject was Bible class, and in school, it was my easiest subject to pass. As early as I can recall, I felt the presence of a spirit next to me. I would always talk with the spirit. Some would call it an imaginary friend, but that friend stayed with me until I was sixteen years old. I never saw whether the spirit was masculine or feminine in gender, but the presence was that of a male. That spirit was my companion and my friend— at least that is what I believed. Stories are often told of children who are alone and make up imaginary friends to talk with, but this was different. I was aware of the spirit, but I never knew if it was an evil spirit until I got older. From the time I was small, I felt the presence of the evil spirit and God's spirit. I guess I was fooled because the devil knows how to look like an angel of light. "And no wonder, for even Satan disguises himself as an angel of light" (2 Corinthians 11:14).

3

Fear

When I was sixteen, something happened that caused me to be afraid for the first time in my life. You see, all my years of growing up, I was brave and bold, not fearful of evil spirits. One day I went to clean my great-grandmother's tomb, and the sun was so hot I decided to sit on top of the tombstone and lay my head on the headstone. Hours later, I woke up. It was night. I found myself in the middle of the graveyard. Unafraid, I got up and left.

When I got home to my grandmother's house, she said, "We looked for you for hours. Where have you been?" I told her while I was cleaning around the tomb, imagining what it would be like to have met her. I got tired and fell asleep.

Whenever my relatives would come from Canada or the United States, they would bring me to the other villages with them because they were afraid to pass the burial grounds they had to pass if they were going to town. We didn't have any streetlights at that time, so we used flashlights. But sometimes I did not have one. No one ever knew why I was not afraid, but the truth is, I always talked with God and sang songs all the way out of the village and back, whether it was raining or not.

But one day in my mother's kitchen in America, I became afraid. A chill came over me while I was washing dishes. Then I felt the presence of an unfamiliar spirit, and it startled me. I had no idea what the spirit was doing. Suddenly, I felt very afraid. This was when I first encountered fear, when I became afraid.

We must always keep in mind God did not give us the spirit of fear, and he does not sneak up on anyone: "For God hath not given us the spirit of fear; but of power, and of love, and of a sound mind" (2 Timothy 1:7).

4

Feeling Alone

I was living with my mother, Celest, her husband, Carl, and my little brother, Samuel. However, because of the abusive situation at my home, my uncle Akin, with the influence of his wife, Aminatu, took me to live with them and their family in Chicago.

In all my experiences, I would never forget what my grandmother Cymone told me about God. I continued to go to church, but later that year, I left the church because I didn't believe in everything they were teaching. And some of my deepest hurts came from the people who attended this church. I felt like I never belonged there. I left the church and searched for something that was missing from my life. There was no one in my life who told me any different at that time.

At this time, I needed to be properly introduced to Christ to develop a deeper relationship with God. But there was no one who lived it around me. There were definitely many religious people, but no one was walking as a believer. "Having a form of godliness but denying its power" (2 Timothy 3:5).

Yes, I used to talk with God, and I've had a relationship with him since then. But for me, it wasn't about my relationship with God. It was about my family and my mother. At the time, Celest wasn't really a mother to me, and I never had a real father in my life. So those were the missing relationships in my life. As a child, I needed that human connection, which I found with my grandmother and later with my uncle, each in their own ways. They did the best they could have done at the time.

I felt alone in the world for a very long time, even though Jesus said, "I will never leave thee, nor forsake thee" (Hebrews 13:5). This was not clear to me at that time, and it doesn't mean that you won't ever feel alone. However, understanding what he is saying gives you strength to go through times when you feel alone.

Knowing that at some point in all our lives we will have these feelings helps us to be strong. Knowing the Word and how to apply it in these times is especially effective. In his Word, he said, "He will not fail thee, nor forsake thee" (Deuteronomy 31:6).

Some people who have single parents feel this way, as do some who have gone through abusive homes, and they don't know where to turn. I know it is only by having a relationship with God that I did not turn to drugs. Some young people who are abused turn to these drugs to fill the void in their lives or to help them cope temporarily. I initially turned to attempting suicide.

Despite all the things I went through while growing up, I continued to read my Bible and pray daily to God because I had developed a relationship with him. There was a lot I still did not understand, but I knew God loved me, and I believed his words. And this is what gave me hope.

From the time I left the church until the age of twenty-three, I experienced some things that made me cling to the Word of God even more.

5

At Sixteen, Fall in Love

At the age of sixteen, even though I had left the church, I continued to study the Bible. I was now living in Chicago with my uncle and his family, and I began to see a young man named Sonny. I had met him through Akin while I was living with Celest. I was warned about his background by a cousin of his and to be careful because they had different beliefs from mine. But I overlooked that part about him because he was a wonderful person, a bodybuilder, and extremely handsome. Besides, nothing out of the ordinary had happened since we started seeing each other. I was naive. I had never had a relationship other than a friendship with someone I had deep feelings for as a thirteen-year-old. And a few crushes.

Sonny was three years older than me and much more experienced. It was new and exciting. I was asked a lot of questions, and we spoke quite often about the things that happened in our lives. There were some things he told me about myself that I never told anyone before, such as being raped. I didn't know what to say about that, but I found him fascinating. And I was intrigued by him.

He was very talented and gifted in all the areas I was interested in for a guy—and more. He was special, and he became the person I wanted to marry. I fell in love with Sonny because he had a wonderful personality, was well rounded in intellect and physique, was easy to converse with, and was respectful. Also, his self-control was impeccable, and he taught me a lot of things—good and bad.

One time I went to see him, and he was meditating. I stood outside the door, and after a while he told me to come in. I asked him what he was doing, and he asked, "Are you sure you want to know?"

I replied, "Yes, I want to know what you are doing. Is it something bad?"

He said no and began to explain what he was doing. But at the time, I still did not understand what I was getting myself into. He taught me a lot about prayers and spiritual things I did not know before. He became my spiritual adviser and best friend for a long time. Sonny taught me about the other side of the spiritual realm, how to palm read, the significance of praying, what to use when praying, and how to meditate. He taught me how to pray for love of someone you desire to be yours. He told me what my astrological sign was and which candles and incense I should use to pray. Sonny told me always to mediate and pray each day, and I would be fine.

We became spiritually bonded without me realizing it. He had led me into the arms of the enemy, and I did not know it. I was so blinded by love that I did not know the warning signs, what to stay away from, and what to denounce. It seemed all so innocent. "For we wrestle not against flesh and blood, but against principalities, against powers, against the rulers of the darkness of this world, against spiritual wickedness in high places" (Ephesians 6:12).

The church I used to attend taught me nothing about fighting spiritual battles and battling the enemy, what to look out for or stay away from, or what to pray for and what to pray against. I loved God, but I was void of the knowledge of what I was facing. So far I had practiced witchcraft, soothsaying, idolatry, debauchery, and fornication. I am pretty sure there were many more. The only one that stood out was fornication because that was the one I did know about among the general sins, such as lying, which I did not practice. The Word of God said, "My people are destroyed for lack of knowledge" (Hosea 4:6a).

The enemy is crafty, and if he does not get you one way, he will try another way. And he will keep trying; he does not stop. I can tell you that until I reread this book, I did not realize I still did not know how much trouble I was really in and why I had been drawn to men who worship the devil.

Palm reading is one way the soothsayers foretell the future, which is against God. "And I will cut off the cities of thy land, and throw down all thy strong holds: and thou shalt have no more soothsayers" (Micah 5:11–12b). In my spiritual walk with God, I learned the only thing we should be mediating on is God's Word, and we must focus on our relationship with him. "This book of the law shall not depart out of thy mouth; but thou shalt meditate therein day and night, that thou mayest observe to do according to all that is written therein: for then thou shalt make thy way prosperous and then thou shalt have good success" (Joshua 1:8).

6

The Root of It All

One day I sat praying and trying to figure out why it was that I only met and dated men who had connections to the devil. I found it must have had something to do with my childhood, who my father is, or what I encountered when I was a child. Without looking too hard, it is rumored that my father practiced witchcraft to acquire wealth and women. It is commonly practiced in the Caribbean Islands as well as many places in the United States and around the world.

It started when I was a child, even before I met my first husband, but I did not realize it. So I will start by saying I was fascinated with other religions since I was a little girl. I did not believe the religion of my grandmother and all that was taught to me. I did not believe that all people who worship on Sundays are Sunday devils and worship the sun, which is often taught to children of that faith growing up in my country, among other things. The question always lingered about how God could only love people who worship on Saturdays since he created all people. My curiosity began an investigation. It began by peeping in the windows of all the churches to see what they were about. Then I would ask adults questions, which would be followed by a spanking for peeping.

There was one church in particular that I should have never looked in the window. My little brother, Obasi, and sister, Amara, were with me on our way home. The spiritual church was having their service, and the three of us peeped in the windows to see what the service was about. They saw us and told us to come into the church. Obasi was not as trusting, but Amara and I were, so we entered the church. They took us to the front of the room and anointed us. I felt funny, but I did not know what had happened, and I thought nothing of it. Then we just went home.

This church was not an ordinary church. It was derived from the Merikins, an enslaved population who engaged in African rituals of sorcery and divinations, and had knowledge of black arts—charms and obeah. I had no idea what I had gotten myself into.

Sonny and I met in late August 1987, but it seemed like a lifetime. He was on vacation and had to leave in December and go back to the Caribbean. I was devastated and lost; I had made him my whole life without realizing it, and when he left, I wanted to die. I saw no reason for living, and I attempted to end my life. I was vulnerable and started to seek worship with others, but I did not find anyone. I began to lose myself; I started spending all my time at nightclubs. I was in my eleventh year in high school, and my grades plummeted from As to Cs and Ds. I cried and drank wine and wine coolers every weekend. My uncle had a big bottle of wine in the house, and within a few months, the bottle was almost gone.

When I stopped drinking, I started praying ritualistically every night. I used red and white candles, incense, and a picture of my boyfriend. I meditated on what I wanted to ask God for. I prayed and cried because in my mind, he was my life, and I wanted to marry him. I couldn't imagine my life anymore without him being in it. I had opened a door to idol worshipping and didn't even know it. "Wherefore, my dearly beloved, flee from idolatry" (1 Corinthians 10:14). Never let anyone be your reason for living. God should be your only reason for living because he will give you directions and a purpose for living. A man cannot give you a purpose for living because he is trying to find out the purpose God has for his life.

Bernie called Sonny and told him of my behavior. Sonny told me I needed to be strong, move on with my life, and not wait for him. And I had to pull my grades up and continue with my school activities. Bernie said, "I don't know what else to say to you."

She asked me if I wanted to be a drunk. And that's when it finally hit me. I thought, *A drunk?* Then I remembered what it said about drunkenness in the Bible, and replied, "I don't want to be a drunk." "But now I have written unto you not to keep company, if any man that is called a brother be a drunkard" (1 Corinthians 5:11f).

I decided to find someone to study the Bible with, so I started studying and praying each day. I wrote Sonny quite often, and he offered advice, especially about trusting strangers because he thought I trusted people too easily. I started seeking to fill the void in my life. One day I was in the kitchen washing dishes, and

I smelled a horrific odor. and I asked, "Bernie, do you smell that horrific odor? It smells like death."

"How does death smell?" she asked. And as I was about to tell her, she said, "Never mind. Just keep your creepy things to yourself." I burst out laughing.

I hope no one dies, was the thought that entered my mind after the laughter was over. Then I got this spooky feeling about the horrific smell.

I remembered R. C., a high school boy I'd dated for a while in tenth grade. I tried to get him to talk about being adopted by a Caucasian family, but he never really wanted to speak much about it. I knew it bothered him, but he always changed the topic to talk about my situation at home. We couldn't see each other much, but we saw each other between classes and after school because he was the school's best football player and track runner. I guess we were drawn to each other because we both had problems at home and we both were on the track team and very athletic. I believe he used sports as a way out, like I did. I know he injured himself just before he graduated, but he already had so many scholarships because he was a model student. I didn't keep in regular contact with him after I left Chicago. We had decided to be friends before I moved to Arlington, and he had another girlfriend.

Nevertheless, I was thinking about him and tried to reach him the whole week and couldn't. Then my girlfriend from Chicago called me and told me she had been trying to reach me because she had some bad news. I asked if it was about R. C., and she said yes. My heart started to race, and she said told me he was dead. I said, "Stop joking like that."

"Why would I joke about something so serious?" Then I started crying, and she said, "I tried to reach you to come to the funeral, but I couldn't."

"How did he die?"

"He hanged himself. They found him in his basement at home."

I walked around in a daze for a while, wondering, *If I had only gotten in contact with him, maybe I could have said something to change his mind because I had an idea what he was going through.*

I felt scared of the horrific smell even more. My aunt said, "I am sorry about your friend, but please don't smell that smell around me." His death affected me a great deal, and I was depressed for a long time.

Bernie said there was nothing I could have done about R. C.'s death and to stop blaming myself and move on. "Being depressed about it is not going to change him being gone."

It took me a while to get over his death, but I eventually did get over the hurt. He was the first boy I danced with, connected with, and became friends with after I came to America. He never tried to have sex with me; we never even talked about it. We just liked to dance, though he had two left feet, which made me laugh all the time. He really was a nice and very handsome young man. I prayed that God would forgive him because he didn't make the right choice about killing himself.

When I was in the same situation, I did the same thing, and God saved me. R. C. told me that his adopted parents were really good to him and made sure he had everything he needed. But he just couldn't cope, I guess because he told me he wanted to find his birth parents one day. I told him I felt the same way before I met my mother. That was as far as the conversation got, but you could tell he was hurting. The feeling of not being wanted by your birth parents could be devastating and deadly.

Another reason might have been because he might not have been able to play ball or run track anymore. I know that he lived to do both, and they kept his mind off everything else. It hurt thinking about it because it could have very well been me. I really wished he had gotten to meet his birth parents. I believe it would have made a big difference in his life.

Many people are adopted and seek to meet their birth parents. It always feels like you are missing who you really are, and the expectation of meeting them is both a good and bad feeling. R. C. was the only one I met who was adapted at that time. I saw how it affected him. It gave him a drive to want to be his best at everything just to feel wanted. This is no way for someone to feel. Feeling like you are not wanted is a familiar feeling for me, and it drives you to do good; it can also drive you to do bad. It is the escape that makes it worthwhile, just knowing that you have a way out. Whether it is a good choice or not, it comforts you and takes your mind of everything you need to face for a while. Some children and adults turn to drugs, alcohol, and prostitution, and all of it leads to death; some methods are just slower than others.

Well I learned that even if you feel no one wants you or loves you, God wants you and loves you. He paid a precious price just to prove that to us: "For God so loved the world that he gave his only begotten Son that whosoever believeth in him shalt not perish but everlasting life" (St. John 3:16). It is the best feeling in the world to know that someone loves you so much that he or she sacrificed everything for you. No one can take that from you. Just knowing this brings about a different outlook on life.

7

The Recruiters: An Encounter with a Cult

Later the year after my love Sonny had left, I went to school in the morning and worked in the evenings. It was my last year in high school, and I was working at Sammy's Drug Store, only about seven minutes from home. I got off at 8:00 p.m. on weekdays and 6:00 p.m. on weekends.

One night while I was leaving I saw this couple in front of the store. When I went outside I greeted them. Then I stopped to chat with a young man I was acquainted with and had not seen for some time. We chatted for about ten minutes, and then I took off for home. As I was going down the hill toward my home, I ran into the same couple I greeted outside my job. It appeared as though they were waiting for someone. I didn't think anything of it, but as I was about to cross the street, they were in my path in front of me. The man said, "Hi. You are the young lady we met up the street earlier. After I told him yes, he asked, "Can we speak with you for a minute?"

"OK. Are you lost or waiting for someone?" I asked because I had never seen them before that night. They said no, so I asked, "Do you live around here?" They told me they lived just across the street. "Well, I am pretty familiar with most of the neighbors, but I had never seen you."

"We are quite busy," they replied.

"Oh, OK. That explains never seeing you around here before."

The man said, "It can be dangerous for a young lady to be walking home around this time." I told them I always prayed that God will protect me. And I walk very fast. When the woman asked if I went to church, I told her, "I haven't gone in a while."

"Well, you can come and study with us sometimes, the woman said, and I said I would.

The man was about six feet four or taller and very black in complexion. The woman was about five feet nine and light skinned. She stretched out her hand to introduce herself. He then held out his hand and introduced himself. But he held my hand and said, "Let me tell you how much I know about you." And he began to tell me all about myself. It reminded me of what Sonny told me about palm reading.

"OK, it was nice meeting you both." They wrote down their information on a piece of paper and told me that I shouldn't walk home by myself because it wasn't safe.

The Bible says, "And no marvel; for Satan himself is transformed into an angel of light" (2 Corinthians 11:14). Those thoughts were not in my mind at the time because the couple had appealed to my emptiness and desire to be connected to God. I was pleased to see how concerned they were for my well-being. And even though my guard was up because I was thinking of what Sonny had told me—"Don't trust people so easily"—because of their concern for my well-being, I was happy to have people to study the Bible with, and I went home excited.

I called Sonny and spoke with him about the new people I met and would study the Bible and worship with, and I told him the scriptures they had given me to study. His advice was, "If they offer you anything to eat or drink, don't take it." He continued, "There is nothing wrong with studying the Bible, but just pay close attention to everything they say in between and what they do. And don't participate in any ritualistic things if that comes up."

I wrote him and told him everything that was going on. I told him about the wonderful food and drinks they offered me, but I told them no and just drank some water at the first Bible study meeting. We studied the Old Testament, and then we prayed, and I went home.

After two weeks, I had gotten quite well acquainted with them, and since they seemed to feel that they had gained my trust, they began to anoint my head with a special oil. They told me that we are one brothers and sisters for life. and no one would ever break this bond; I am one of them now. By this time my guard was up again, but I didn't make them aware of it. I wanted to know what they meant when they said that I am their brother and sister for life and I am one of them now. I know this one thing: If you are earnestly seeking God's guidance and are lacking knowledge, you can fall for the enemy's traps easier. But God knows you hear him and the plans he has for you. In his Word he said, "The Lord also will be a refuge for the oppressed, a refuge in times of trouble" (Psalm 9:9).

Despite my questioning, I continued to study and pray with them. But I also prayed and asked God to show me if they were not of him I could stop studying with them. The enemy is crafty and can use the Bible for his crafty works because the enemy knows the Bible much more than you or me. The enemy is always plotting to take out the children of God, and I believe if I did not give my life to Jesus at the age of twelve and had a relationship with him, I might not be writing this story to warn you today: "But I was like a lamb or an ox that is brought to the slaughter; and I knew not that they had devised devices against me, saying, Let us destroy the tree with the fruit thereof, and let us cut him off from the land of the living, that his name may be no more remembered" (Jeremiah 11:19).

The couple told me always to pray eastward each night and to wear a white garment and tie or wrap my head with something white. I did just what they told me to do. I always studied the Bible after I left them and prayed additionally.

8

After the Encounter: The Recruiters' Plan Exposed

My uncle Akin became upset about where I was spending my time. The couple told me not to tell my family that we were meeting for Bible study. I thought that was very strange because when people study the Bible, they are so excited about it, they don't mind telling their families. That is, unless they are forbidden because of their families' beliefs are other than Christianity.

I was seventeen, and I talked with Bernie about most everything. She became my mentor when I moved in with my uncle Akin, so I thought it would be best to tell her. And when I did, she said, "Be careful. Something just doesn't sit right with me about these people." Well, speaking with Bernie confirmed my concerns. I told her my only purpose in studying with these people was my relationship with God and not to get involved in any evil works. I would just keep praying and trusting God. Eventually Akin and Bernie started complaining about the oil the couple was using to anoint my head each time we met for Bible study.

The couple told me the job I had was not good enough for me, and I could do better. And if I wanted anything, to let them know and we would pray for it. I just needed to believe that I would have it, and whatever it was would be mine. So I told them what job I wanted, and I got it!

They also told me that I would become a prostitute if I didn't change my direction in life. I was really puzzled because I was not even dating anyone. They said, "Well we see it in you."

They wanted me to read Ezekiel chapter 23. As I begin to read it, which deals with Samaria and Jerusalem committing whoredoms against God, I became increasingly puzzled and a bit offended. But I continued to study the Bible with them.

Then one night they offered me some water, and I said no. I was not thirsty. The man told me that the woman was going to stand behind me and catch me because I was going to fall backward as we stood to pray. I chuckled and said that they were joking but OK. The man sprinkled some water on my forehead, and I fell backward; she caught me. I must admit I was a bit spooked and planned on not seeing them again. But they asked me to pray eastward tonight and I agreed.

I left their apartment, which was on the top floor of the building, and went home across the street. When I got home, I took a shower, dressed in my white, and started praying eastward. I knew Psalm 23 by heart; my grandmother had taught it to me and told me to always repeat the Lord's Prayer. As I began to pray, I asked God to reveal the enemy's plans if they were not of him so that I could stop having Bible study with them if they were not of him. As I continued to pray, I saw a pentagram with a fire in the middle. There were five shadows around the fire, one at each corner. They appeared to be praying. One of them left the fire and came toward me, so I opened my eyes. The more earnestly I prayed, the closer it came toward me. I started crying and praying Psalm 23 and our Father's Prayer, and then it disappeared. I thank God for saving my life. I eventually fell off to sleep. God had revealed their intentions to take my soul that night.

That night my little cousin saw the same things, even though he was not in the room. I quit my job and found one closer to home. And I started taking a different path home.

My aunt told me she saw the man just standing on the sidewalk, looking at my apartment building for some time. But I never saw them. After about a month, I saw them in my line where I was working. I tried to avoid them, but they persisted in order to speak with me. I came out from behind the counter and spoke with them. The man said to me, "You are a very strong person, but you will be our sister for life."

I replied, "We are not brothers and sisters. Have a great day, and please do not come to my job anymore."

9

Attempting to Move On

How many of you know that when the enemy realizes he is defeated, he will try to take you out another way. I started getting attacks when I turned eighteen years old, each time after I fell off to sleep at night. My family became fearful, but they did not stop. As soon as I fell asleep, I would be choked and pinned down to the bed so I could not move.

I started dating this young man whom I loved very much. I thought we were going to get married after dating for a while. But then some things happened in our relationship, and I broke it off. We would still see each other, and one day we made a date to go out. When he did not show up, I went to his apartment, and we spoke for some time. He kept telling me that I was too sweet, but he wanted us to reconnect with each other, so we made another plan to go out again. As I left his apartment, we kissed and said goodbye. But he looked at me as if it was goodbye forever. I told him, "Don't do that. You are acting like I am never going to see you again."

Later my aunt asked me to invite him to Thanksgiving, and

I said that would be great. I tried to reach him, but when I did not get any answers after a while. I said, "Let me call his mother."

His cousin picked up the phone and said, "We have been trying to reach you for a while now. Tendaji is dead, and we buried him last week. He and his friend got into an argument over some money owed to them, and one shot him in the head. The man who was supposed to be his best friend is believed to have let them in and was a part of it." I was devastated and wanted to die because I thought it was somehow my fault because I messed with these people.

10

Man becomes Idol

I never stopped talking to Sonny, so I called him and told him what had taken place. We were joking one day, and he said, "OK, by the time I am twenty-four years old, if we are not married, we will get married to each other. I agreed, so I poured all my love, dreams, and hope into him once again.

I started practicing some of the things he taught me about using different methods of praying for someone I loved. To be honest, I thought it was all innocent. I had tied myself to him and did not even know it. It turned out to be the worst thing I ever did because I ended up seeing things that he was doing and feeling things he felt. I automatically knew when something was wrong with him before anyone else knew, and no one had to call me to tell me what was going on with him. His friends and uncle started calling me a witch, saying I practiced witchcraft. I denied it, and I never kept anything from him because he knew. We joked about it, and he said there was nothing wrong with it. This man had become my god. No one could say anything bad about him without me defending him. Not even his family.

11

The Power of Prayer

Regarding our weaknesses, Jesus said that he would send the Comforter:

> Blessed be God, even the Father of our Lord Jesus
> Christ, the Father of mercies, and the God of all
> comfort; Who comforteth us in all our tribulation,
> that we may be able to comfort them which are in
> any trouble, by the comfort wherewith we ourselves
> are comforted of God; (2 Corinthians 1:3–4)

During the time I was mourning Tendaji's death, I got really sick and had an out-of-body experience. My spirit left my body and went to what I believe to be hell. I was guided by a spirit, and I asked a lot of questions along the way. I asked about the people on the first level of hell and the second level, and about the bottomless pit of what I saw. The spirit beckoned me to go further down to the first level of hell. I said no and ran back. Then I awoke. Later that day I called and told Sonny, who said I should go back to see more. I told him OK, but I said to myself, *Nope, I am never going there again. It was horrible.* What I saw was real. People were being tormented and were crying out to God. I remembered at one point the spirit warned me, "Don't let them see you."

As the years went by, Sonny helped me thorough Tendaji's death and every other obstacle I faced. It cost me thousands of dollars because after we got married, I took care of all his financial needs. And when I neglected to do so, he threw a tantrum.

The Bible says, "Thus saith the Lord; Cursed be the man that trusteth in man, and maketh flesh his arm, and whose heart departeth from the Lord" (Jeremiah 17:5). I had put my trust in man instead of God and, therefore, brought curses upon myself without even knowing it. "My people are destroyed for lack of knowledge: because thou hast rejected knowledge, I will also reject thee, that thou shalt be no priest to me: seeing thou hast forgotten the law of thy God, I will also forget thy children" (Hosea 4:6).

I would leave myself undone to make sure he had what he needed.

12

Surrendering to the Lord

The attacks kept on coming, and it was driving me up the walls. But I continued to pray. I was still not living for God. I am a loyal bus catcher, and for about two months, each time I sat in a seat, there was a track or a pamphlet waiting for me saying, "Repent and be baptized." I kept putting it off, even with this happening. I asked the people on the bus if they had received a track as well, and they all told me no.

I was stricken once again with the flu. But it seemed worse than the flu, so I went to bed on Saturday night, September 11, 1993, and by the next day, it had gotten worse. The Holy Spirit had awakened me because I heard a voice tell me to get up and go to church. The first time I turned around and went back to sleep. The voice said to me again to get up and go to church. And I went back to sleep again. The third time the Holy Spirit told me to get up and go to church. I said, "Lord, I know that it is you, but I don't go to church on Sundays. But I will go." The area in which I lived had a church on each corner, so I got myself together, put on one of my best suits—black-and-white pinstripe with gold in it—with my black hose, black-and-gold necklace watch, and matching earrings and bracelet. I asked, "Lord, what church should I go to? I need you to show me." Then I can say the Lord brought to my memory a Baptist church to my right, about half a block away across the street. "I will go to that one," I said.

I went in the side entrance and sat in the front. When the minister offered salvation, I went up front, gave my life to the Lord, and was baptized that very day. As soon as I was baptized, the sickness went away. And according to a friend, a glow came over me. My life has never been the same.

13

Strongholds

I was still single, so I called Sonny and asked him if he was serious about the promise we had made. He said yes, so we planned the wedding. I went to meet him, and we got married.

Little did I know there was more trouble waiting for me. The night of our wedding, my husband said that he was going out for a bit. He didn't return for hours. I was devastated and began to drink. I had gone to the store to get some wine coolers, but at the time, I did not know the difference between spirits and wine coolers. I ended up drinking the whole bottle of rum—straight. All I knew was that I was being beaten up in the spirit, tormented, and dragged. I called on Jesus the whole time because I did not know what I had gotten myself into. I did not remember anything except for that. They told me I made a mess all over myself, and they gave me a bath and dressed me. When I opened my eyes, I was at the airport headed back to the United States.

My husband had come home, and they brought me to the airport. He gave me a cup of coffee, but the people at the airport said I could not fly back because I was too intoxicated. My husband gave me a lecture and apologized for not coming back that night.

I finally boarded the plane the next day, after paying an additional amount for one additional day. I could not believe all that had taken place. In 2009 I eventually filed for a divorce, against his wishes, because he had cheated on me. The distance between us might have played a part in it.

I have continued to live my life for God. Even though I have fallen many times, I was able to get up and get back in line with God's Word. One of the key scriptures that I live by is, "For we wrestle not against flesh and blood, but against principalities, against powers, against the rulers of the darkness of this world, against spiritual wickedness in high places" (Ephesians 6:12).

My hope and prayer is that we continue to win as many souls as we can for Christ before our journey here on earth is over. If there is no purpose in my living, then I won't be here.

I will continue to share my testimony with whoever has an open ear and heart to receive it, so they can truly see that no matter how dim or bleak a situation looks, God is still in control.

It has been my joy to write this book. And I give God all the glory.

About the Author

The author is a mother, a full-time civil servant, and is currently pursuing to become a business owner of natural skincare products. She was an outreach minister for over ten years, successfully bridging the gap between the local churches and the communities.

She has received several awards as a writer. She spent the first thirteen and a half years of her life in the Sunny Island. She moved to the United States at the age of thirteen and has been here ever since. Over the years she has received many certificates for teaching and being a church leader.

Lightning Source UK Ltd.
Milton Keynes UK
UKHW010717120821
388748UK00001B/112